International Trade
A Case Study

Nicolas Brasch

Australia • Brazil • Japan • Korea • Mexico • Singapore • Spain • United Kingdom • United States

International Trade: A Case Study

Fast Forward
Gold Level 21

Text: Nicolas Brasch
Editor: Cameron Macintosh
Design: Stella Vassiliou
Series design: James Lowe
Production controller: Seona Galbally
Photo research: Fiona Smith
Audio recordings: Juliet Hill, Picture Start
Spoken by: Matthew King and Abbe Holmes

Acknowledgements
The author and publisher would like to acknowledge permission to reproduce material from the following sources: Photographs by AAP Image/AFP Photo/Greg Wood, pp front cover centre, 1 centre, 21; Alamy/cameraPT, p 22; Corbis/Justin Guariglia, p 20; Fairfaxphotos/Penny Bradfield, p 5; Getty Images/Stone/David Sacks, p 17; iStockphoto.com/Jenny Solomon, p 7 bottom; Newspix/AFP Photo/Yoshikazu Tsuno, pp front cover bottom left, 1 bottom left, 19; Newspix/John Feder, p 23; Photolibrary/ Alamy/Horizon International Images Limited/Milton Wordley, p 14; Photolibrary/George Hall, p 16; Photolibrary/Gillianne Tedder, p 18; Photolibrary/ JTB Photo Communications Inc, p 9; Photolibrary/Neil Duncan, p 7 top; Photolibrary/ Science Photo Library/John Mead, p 15; Photolibrary/Superstock, Inc/Douglas Armand, p 8; Photolibrary/ Workbook, Inc/Marc Romanelli, p 4.

ISBN 978 0 17 012676 2
ISBN 978 0 17 012669 4 (set)

Cengage Learning Australia
Level 7, 80 Dorcas Street
South Melbourne, Victoria Australia 3205
Phone: 1300 790 853

Cengage Learning New Zealand
Unit 4B Rosedale Office Park
331 Rosedale Road, Albany, North Shore NZ 0632
Phone: 0800 449 725

For learning solutions, visit **cengage.com.au**

Printed in Australia by Ligare Pty Ltd
5 6 7 8 9 10 11 20 19 18 17 16

THE UNIVERSITY OF MELBOURNE

Evaluated in independent research by staff from the Department of Language, Literacy and Arts Education at the University of Melbourne.

International Trade
A Case Study

Nicolas Brasch

Contents

Chapter 1

RUNNING A HOUSEHOLD

For a household to run well, it needs to earn more money than it spends. Otherwise, it will run out of money.

Countries are the same. Countries sell goods to other countries to earn money.

No country can produce everything that its people need and want, so each country spends money buying goods from other countries.

trade talks between Australia and Japan, 2005

Japan and Australia are two countries that buy what they need from each other.

Chapter 2

AUSTRALIA AND JAPAN

Australia and Japan are very different countries. Australia is very large, while Japan is quite small. Few people live in Australia, while a lot of people live in Japan.

Australia's land is quite flat.
Japan is hilly and mountainous.

the Australian countryside

Mount Fuji, Japan

Australia is isolated from other countries, while Japan is located close to many other countries.

All of these these differences make Australia and Japan suitable trading partners.

Fact File: Japan

Capital city: Tokyo

Population: 127 400 000

Land area: 374 744 square kilometres

Highest point: Mount Fuji at 3776 metres

Value of **exports** in 2005: US$550 billion

Value of **imports** in 2005: US$450 billion

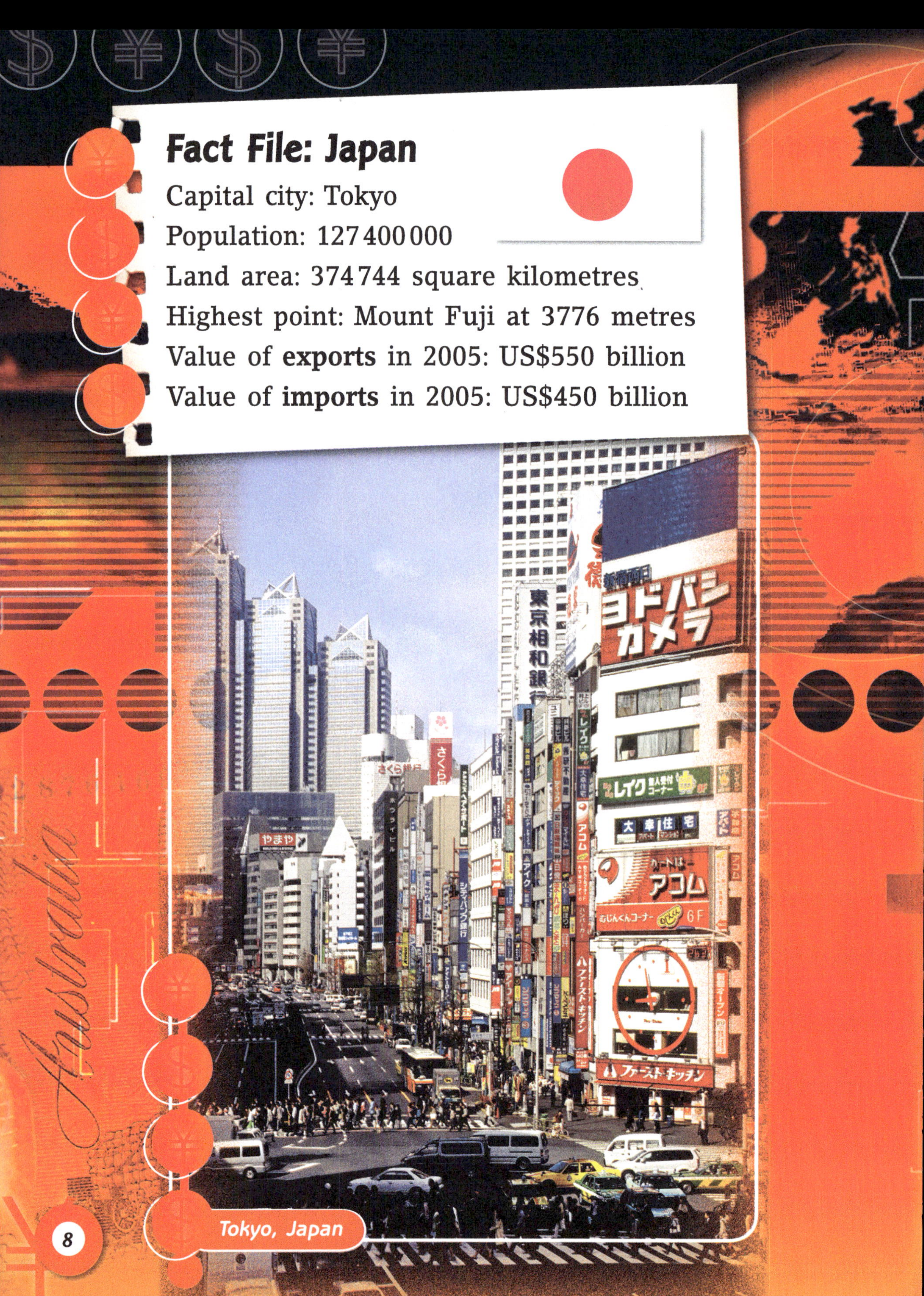

Tokyo, Japan

Fact File: Australia

Capital city: Canberra

Population: 20 100 000

Land area: 7 617 930 square kilometres

Highest point: Mount Kosciuszko, at 2229 metres

Value of exports in 2005: US$103 billion

Value of imports in 2005: US$119 billion

EXPORTING AND IMPORTING

Selling goods to another country is called exporting. Australia and Japan export goods to each other, and to many other countries as well.

In order, Japan's five main export destinations are:

- the United States of America
- China
- the Republic of Korea
- Taiwan
- Hong Kong.

Running Words: 242

In order, Australia's five main export destinations are:

- Japan
- China
- the Republic of Korea
- the United States of America
- New Zealand.

Buying goods from another country is called importing. Australia and Japan import goods from each other and from many other countries as well.

In order, Japan's five main import sources are:

- China
- the United States of America
- the Republic of Korea
- Australia
- Indonesia.

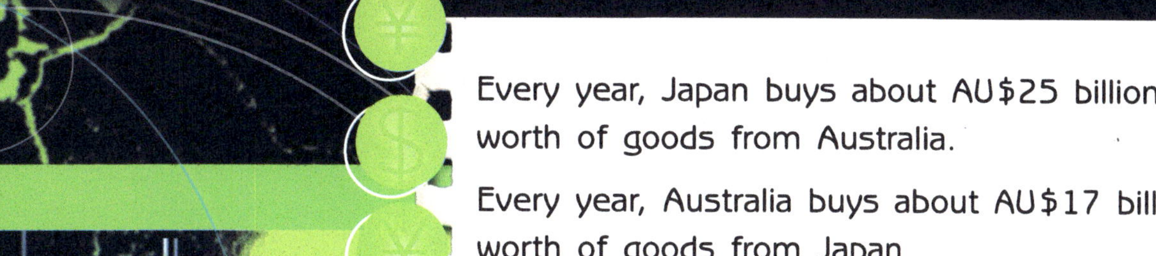

Every year, Japan buys about AU$25 billion worth of goods from Australia.

Every year, Australia buys about AU$17 billion worth of goods from Japan.

In order, Australia's five main import sources are:

- the United States of America
- China
- Japan
- Germany
- Singapore.

Chapter 4

MINERALS

Australia has a lot of minerals under the ground,
and they are quite easy to mine.
Japan does not have a mining industry of its own.
Japan's hills and mountains
make it too hard to mine the minerals
that may be underground.

So Australia sells minerals to Japan.

gold mining in Australia

The main minerals and metals Australia sells to Japan are coal, iron ore and aluminium.

Australia sells more coal to Japan than any other mineral.
In fact, coal is Australia's major export to Japan.
In 2004–2005, Australia sold more than AU$7 billion worth of coal to Japan.

Australian coal being put onto a ship for export

Japan uses Australian coal to produce electricity that lights and heats Japanese homes and powers Japanese factories.

Chapter 5

AGRICULTURAL PRODUCTS

Australia has a very large **agricultural** industry. This is because Australia's land and climate are suitable for producing particular crops and breeding particular animals. Australia produces more than enough agricultural products to feed its population because Australia has a small population.

Japan has a small agricultural industry. This is because there is not much land suitable for producing crops and breeding animals. But Japan has a large population to feed, so Australia sells agricultural products to Japan. The main agricultural product that Australia sells to Japan is beef. In 2004–2005, Australia sold more than AU $2.6 billion worth of beef to Japan.

Chapter 6

MOTOR VEHICLES

Australia has a small motor vehicle industry.
It is not large enough to supply motor vehicles to all the Australian people and businesses who want one.

Japan has a very large motor vehicle industry.
It has developed technology and introduced ways of working that enable Japan to produce reliable motor vehicles reasonably cheaply.

Australian companies are unable to produce
the same type of motor vehicles
as cheaply as the Japanese companies can.
So Australia imports motor vehicles from Japan.

In 2004–2005, Australia bought more than AU$8 billion worth of motor vehicles from Japan.

Australia also bought more than AU$1 billion worth of motor vehicle parts from Japan. These parts included motors and rubber tyres.

Australian coal is used to power Japanese motor vehicle factories. Australian iron is used in the bodies and parts of the motor vehicles that Japan manufactures. Australian rubber is used in the tyres Japan manufactures.

Japan could not make motor vehicles without the help of Australia. Australians couldn't afford to buy motor vehicles if they didn't make money from the goods they sold to Japan and other countries.

Glossary

agricultural growing plants or rearing animals for food

exports the goods that one country sells to another country

imports the goods that one country buys from another country

Index